6849

Music Minus One Trumpet

ARBAN'S
OPERA ARIAS
FOR
TRUMPET & ORCHESTRA

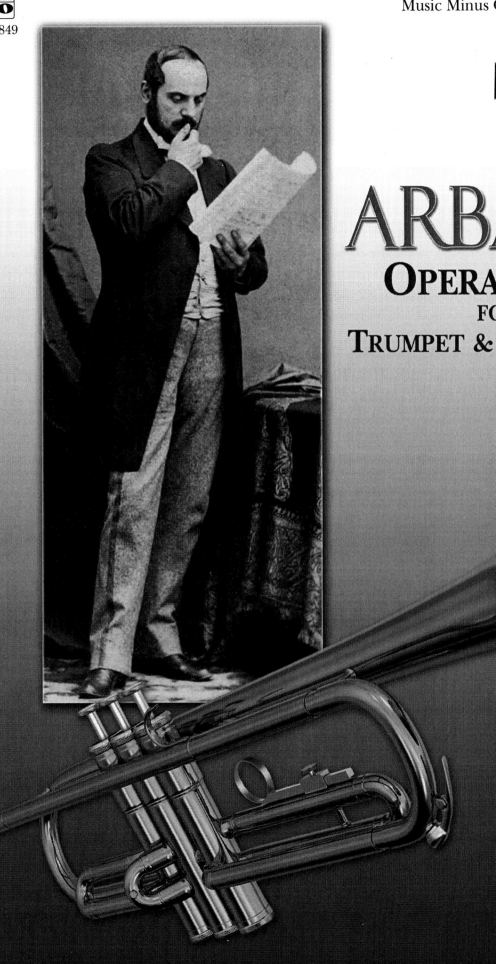

- notes continued from back cover

The epitome of this most fortunate early exposure to operatic arias was with his concert band where he allowed me to play the third cornet parts. I have vivid memories of hearing the solo cornetist playing the thrilling arias from La Boheme and Madame Butterfly!

What was so wonderful about the concert band experience in that era for trumpet players was the special respect given to the solo cornetist role for his chair was actually positioned a small distance from the section! Also, he was not required to play the section parts in order to be "fresh" for the "singing" of the arias! In Italy, these cornet solists were revered by the fans like the adoration given to a Pavarotti or Joan Sutherland!

Ah, the good old days!

This album's focus is to provide a platform for trumpet players to play these beautiful melodies with accompaniment, a luxury that was rarely available when I was a student. One would have to acquire piano scores for these arias and edit and transpose them into the keys that Arban chose for them. Then find a suitable pianist to play them with you. No small undertaking!

Well, that's all done for you here in this collection of 15 from the Arban book with arrangements for virtual orchestra by Jim Odrich a very fine pianist and arranger from New York. And how about this for synchronicity, in the late 1950s, Jim and I were members of the Airmen of Note, the premiere jazz and dance band of the United States Air Force based in Washington, DC which was conducted by the great trombonist/arranger Sam Nestico. This was the same band that starred in the Glenn Miller Story with Jimmy Stewart! And here we are together again creating this MMO more than a half century later!

The first four "bonus" arias were originally recorded for Music Minus One by the Plovdiv Phiharmonic Orchestra conducted by Nayden Todorov for vocal renditions. I edited, arranged and adapted these arias for trumpet to complement the fifteen from the Art of Phrasing.

The plan was to offer accompaniment tracks that approximate the authentic operatic settings of these excerpts along with my renditions all at a very affordable price.

My challenge was to achieve a balance between the operatic vocal approach, in other words, a dramatic interpretation with lots of vibrato and the less stylistic sound of the contemporary symphonic orchestral trumpet player.

Note: When playing with the first four tracks of the Plovdiv Philharmonic Orchestra, you'll need to tune your instrument to the slightly higher pitch used by European orchestras.

Also you'll find that in order to reproduce fermatas, cadenzas and rubato passages with those tracks, you'll have to listen repetitively in order to learn the timing of the orchestra entrances.

With the Arban arias (5-19) we've converted such passages to be timed to an even pulse to facilitate the play-along experience. This, of course affects the notation by adding beats and altering time signatures but shouldn't present an obstacle.

I recommend that you take advantage of hearing the many fine operatic performances of these arias on the internet in order to realize the story and emotional environment. I even considered including the translations of all of the arias titles into English to help you arrive at a more authentic performance. You may pursue that if it interests you or request them from me if you like.

For example, one of the most famous arias in this collection is Verdi's Libiamo Ne'Lieti Calici from La Traviata. This translates as Let's Drink From The Joyful Cups and is actually known as The Drinking Song!

An interesting fact is this type of song is known as a Brindisi which is a lively song that encourages the drinking of wine and other alcoholic beverages!

Never too old to learn something new is my motto!

My wish is that this offering will provide insights and an enhanced enjoyment of operatic music while providing a practical educational tool.

As always, I welcome your comments and questions about this and all my MMOs. In fact, I now offer a complimentary Skype session to give guidance in how to derive the most benefit from my Music Minus One albums.

You may contact me at bobzottolamusic@gmail.com. You can also visit my website www.naplesjazzlovers.com for more information.

All the best!
Bob Zottola
Naples, Florida

ARBAN'S
OPERA ARIAS
FOR TRUMPET & ORCHESTRA

CONTENTS

Complete Track	Minus Track		Page
	20	Bb Tuning Notes	
1	21	La Donna è Mobile	4
2	22	Una Furtiva Lagrima	6
3	23	Di Tanti Palpiti	8
4	24	Merce, Dilette Amici	10
5	25	Quanto è Bella	12
6	26	Sempre Libera	13
7	27	Voilà Donc Le Triste	14
8	28	Oh! Come da Quel di Tutto	15
9	29	Vien Leonora	16
10	30	Mentre Contemplo Quel Volto Amato	17
11	31	O Quante Lacrime Timor	18
12	32	Dell'iniqua, Del Protervo	19
13	33	Or Tutti Sorgete Ministri Infernali	20
14	34	Raggio d'Amor Parea	21
15	35	Come, Innocente Giovane	22
16	36	Meco Tu Vieni	23
17	37	Di Tale Amor che Dirsi	24
18	38	Quando le Sere al Placido	25
19	39	Libiamo Ne'lieti Calici	26

Transcribed by Kevin Mauldin
MMO 6849

La Donna è Mobile

from Rigoletto

Solo Bb Trumpet or Cornet

Guiseppe Verdi
Edited by Robert Zottola

La Donna

Una Furtiva Lagrima

from L'Elisir d'Amore

Solo Bb Trumpet or Cornet

Gaetano Donizetti
Edited by Robert Zottola

This page left blank to facilitate page turns

MMO 6849

Di Tanti Palpiti

from Tancredi

Solo Bb Trumpet or Cornet

Gioachino Rossini
Edited by Robert Zottola

MMO 6849

Di Tanti Palpiti

Merce, Dilette Amici

from I Vespri Siciliani

Solo Bb Trumpet or Cornet

Giuseppe Verdi
Edited by Robert Zottola

Merce, Dilette Amici

Quanto è Bella

from L'elisir D'amore

Solo Bb Trumpet or Cornet

Gaetano Donizetti
Edited by Robert Zottola

Andante

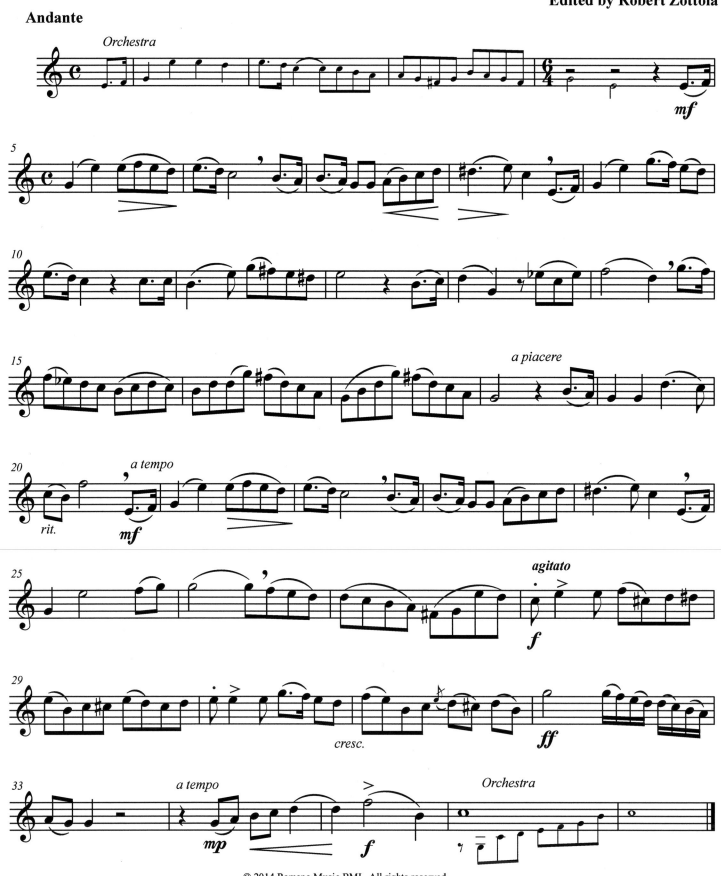

Sempre Libera

from La Traviata

Solo Bb Trumpet or Cornet

Giuseppe Verdi
Edited by Robert Zottola

MMO 6849

Voilà Donc Le Triste

from Gemma Di Vergy

Solo Bb Trumpet or Cornet

Gaetano Donizetti
Edited by Robert Zottola

Oh! Come da Quel di Tutto

from Semiramide

Solo Bb Trumpet or Cornet

Giaochino Rossini
Edited by Robert Zottola

MMO 6849

Vien Leonora

from La Favorita

Solo Bb Trumpet or Cornet

Gaetano Donizetti
Edited by Robert Zottola

Mentre Contemplo Quel Volto Amato

from I Vespri Siciliani

Giuseppe Verdi
Edited by Robert Zottola

Solo Bb Trumpet or Cornet

O Quante Lacrime Timor

From La Donna Del Lago

Gioachino Rossini
Edited by Robert Zottola

Solo Bb Trumpet or Cornet

Dell'iniqua, Del Protervo

from Il Poliuto

Gaetano Donizetti
Edited by Robert Zottola

Solo Bb Trumpet or Cornet

Larghetto

Or Tutti Sorgete Ministri Infernali

from Macbeth

Solo Bb Trumpet or Cornet

Guiseppe Verdi
Edited by Robert Zottola

Allegro maestoso

Raggio d'Amor Parea

from Il Furioso

Solo Bb Trumpet or Cornet

Gaetano Donizetti
Edited by Robert Zottola

Andantino

MMO 6849

Come, Innocente Giovane

from Anna Bolena

Solo Bb Trumpet or Cornet

Gaetano Donizetti
Edited by Robert Zottola

Meco Tu Vieni

from La Straniera

Vincenzo Bellini
Edited by Robert Zottola

Solo Bb Trumpet or Cornet

MMO 6849

Di Tale Amor che Dirsi

from Il Trovatore

Solo Bb Trumpet or Cornet

Guiseppe Verdi

MMO 6849

Quando le Sere al Placido

from Luisa Miller

Guiseppe Verdi
Edited by Robert Zottola

Solo Bb Trumpet or Cornet

MMO 6849

Libiamo Ne'lieti Calici

from La Traviata

Guiseppe Verdi
Edited by Robert Zottola

Solo Bb Trumpet or Cornet

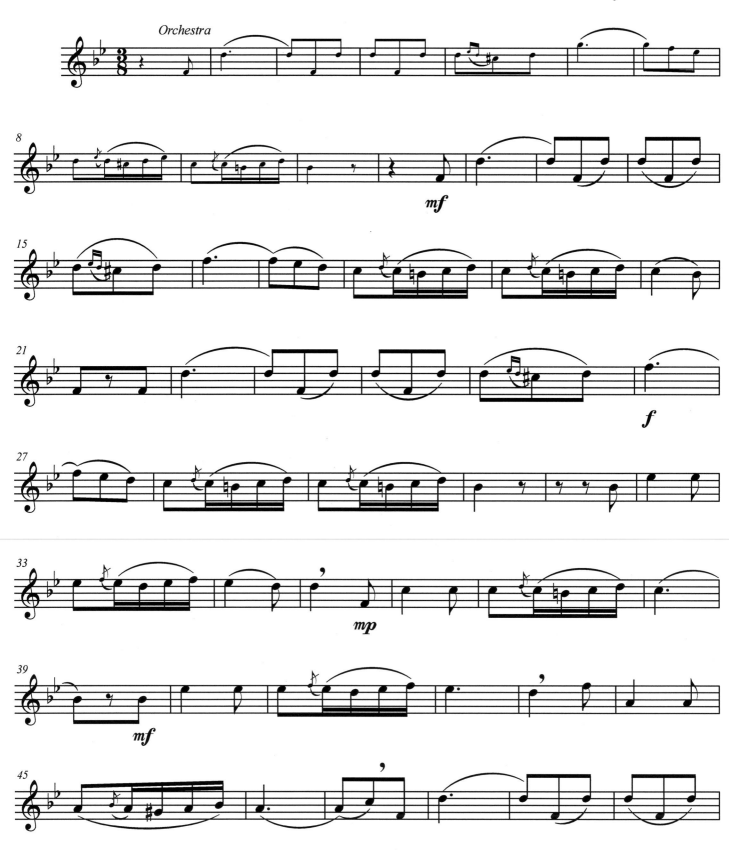

Libiamo Ne'lieti Calici

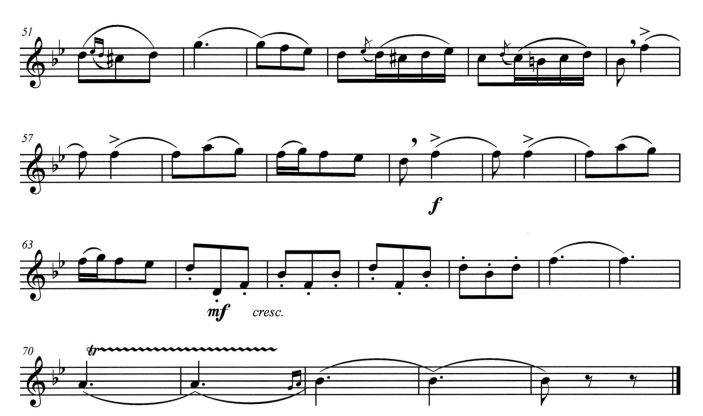

Music Minus One
50 Executive Boulevard • Elmsford, New York 10523-1325
914-592-1188 • e-mail: info@musicminusone.com
www.musicminusone.com

MMO 6849

ISBN 978-0-9916347-2-9